BREAKIN CYCLES

THE POWER OF MY TESTIMONY

TONY V. BUNION JR.

BREAKIN CYCLES

THE POWER OF MY TESTIMONY

This Book Is Dedicated to Our Beautiful Butterfly Baby

MALIA DIONNE BUNION

March 30, 2019 – September 26, 2019

We Will Love You Forever, Our Sweet Baby.

"Love never gives up, never loses faith, is always
hopeful, and endures through every circumstance."
1 Corinthians 13:7

To Whitney, my better half.

Thanks for believing in me. Your unwavering support, advice, and prayers have given me the encouragement to succeed. I would not be the man I am today without your unconditional love. You are my rock. You are my Queen. I'm extremely blessed to have you by my side through life's journeys. You made me a husband, a father, and a greater man. I knew God favored me by allowing me to marry one of His angels.

To Marcus, my only son.

Thank you for being such an amazing son. You are respectful, talented, smart, and outgoing. You are a cycle breaker and no matter what life brings your way, just know you can overcome it. Life can be unfair at times, but I will always believe in you. I need you to always believe in yourself as well. One day I pray you will recognize that I changed my life to give you the chance to live a better life. I am so proud to be your father.

To Maya, my princess.

You will always be my baby girl and I will always love you like no other. You are so full of personality. You are smart, funny, and have such a sweet spirit. You are beautiful inside and outside. Even when I stop holding your hand, I will never stop having your back. Remember to always respect and value yourself or no one else will. I am so honored to call you my daughter.

To Malia, my sweet Butterfly Baby.

Although you were not with us long, your life blessed our lives. You taught us how to love unconditionally. You helped us to realize the importance of having great family support. Despite what you were going through physically, your life was a testament that a butterfly can go through a great deal of darkness and still become something beautiful.

Contents

Foreword

De'Garryan Andrews

love my hometown. There is no place on earth like Havana, Florida. There is much to be said of its southern familial atmosphere. Even visitors feel as if they are coming home. Havana cultivates a sense of pride in its citizens, and we will "rep our town" with a fervor as tenacious as a pack of rabid wolves. Our town has ignited fires in people, like myself and author Tony Bunion Jr., that have allowed us to soar to places and heights we once could only dream about. This is not to say we were impervious to the pitfalls of teen angst, becoming products of most of the environment, or were not tempted by status acquired by illegal means. Havana is an oasis but it is still the real world and we grew up in it.

There is an urgent need for a book like *"Breakin Cycles"*. As an educator, I've sadly seen many young men and women fall into lives of crime, largely due to their home environment.

XII | BREAKIN CYCLES THE POWER OF MY TESTIMONY

It is our responsibility as parents, teachers, coaches, etc. to shape the lives of our youth. It is of paramount importance that we show them there is more out there. This is why Tony is the perfect person to author a book on this sensitive subject matter. Even as a child, I knew there was something underneath Tony's macho bravado. In those moments when he commanded the attention of an entire classroom with his comedic antics, I always knew there was more to his story. I could see a struggle between where he was and where he knew he should go. As a young black man, such a struggle could have proven detrimental. To carry what feels like the weight of the world, to be constantly judged because of where you are from, and to try to live up to your name can all be very daunting. Tony made it out, we all made it out, and he has chosen now to bequeath his testimony to us.

I believe in the power of his testimony. I am grateful that he has decided to share how he navigated through such a perilous upbringing to become the man, husband, and father he is today. It is my sincere prayer that this book is seen as a blueprint for hope, someone reaching back to uplift and inspire. It has certainly done those things for me.

Preface

This book is about my life. It describes how God saved me from my own bad decisions as well as how He used me to break generational cycles in my family. The message and lessons it contains are not for everyone. There's a distinct crowd of people to whom I am writing. It is for those who grew up in poverty, public housing, faced many obstacles within their own families and communities but never gave up. It is for those who are dreamers and refuse to settle for mediocrity. It is for the unprivileged children who have so much potential but no role model or anyone to guide them along the way. This book is for everyone that believes in God's Word and believes He has placed inside of us everything we need to live our best life. It is for those that understand that God will always do His part but we must be accountable also and do our part. I have written this book for those who have been struggling to find their purpose in life, for those who have made some mistakes, and for those who feel trapped in a generational cycle. It is for those who know they were born to do better than what they are currently doing. If you fit into any of the categories above, this book is for YOU.

It is my hope and prayer this book encourages and empowers you to keep moving forward to do all of the things people said you would not accomplish. Don't just believe you can do it. Plan to do it and expect to do it. You are a cycle breaker. *"No eye has seen, no ear has heard, and no mind has imagined what God has prepared for those who love Him".* (1 Corinthians 2:9 NLT).

I desire that this book will motivate the reader to become a better person. It doesn't matter what our race or gender may be, we all need God to improve us and take our lives to higher levels. May you find the positive even in your difficult times because your strength comes from your struggles. I have intentionally shared some intimate and personal details about my family life to inspire others to try God. I assure you if you will establish a better relationship with God He will expand your horizons, and affect your life. His presence will change your life as well as your family's life for generations to come. I pray you will find inspiration from reading my testimony, Breakin Cycles!

Acknowledgments

I t took many years, tears, mistakes, lessons learned, and a whole lot of grace and mercy for this book to reach your hands. I wish to express my gratitude and respect to everyone who provided help, guidance, and prayers during this process. I truly thank my Lord Jesus Christ for sparing my life and using me for His glory. I also want to thank every person who encouraged me on this journey.

To my village: my wife, Dr.Whitney Bunion; my mother-in-law, Dr.Cynthia Griffin; my father-in-law, Rev. Dr.Mark Griffin; my sister-in-law, Minister Crystal Griffin; your support through this journey has been invaluable. Thank you for reading early copies, giving me feedback in both a personal and professional capacity, correcting errors, and helping me to give my readers the best product. I want to thank author and educator Mrs.Betty James, my aunt-in-law for all of your help. To actor and educator Mr.De'Garryan Andrews, thank you for believing in me and supporting me on this journey. This book started with only one writer, but the finished product consisted of many.

I would like to humbly acknowledge my mama, Pamela. Where would I be without you and God? If it was not for you, I would not be here. Thank you for being the strong black woman you are. I know it was not easy for you at times, but you never threw in the towel. You never stopped trying. You are a real-life superwoman. To my pops Tony, Sr.; I truly appreciate the tough love. Thank you for keeping it real with me and nothing less. Thanks for always having my back and teaching me to be a man of my word.

To my grandmothers, I can't thank you enough for loving me and always opening the door for me no matter the time of day or night. I will always be grateful for my Grandma Mattie-May who makes me a pound cake every time I go back home. To my Grandma Essie-May; who is resting in heaven I miss you so much granny-granny. I truly love both of you.

To my grandfathers, Willie and Solomon who are both in heaven; even though I never got the chance to meet either of you, I'm sure you both were amazing men. Thank you for my bloodline, its royalty. To my aunties Mary, Ruthie, Tameka, my aunt in heaven Shelia, my uncles John and Galvin; thank you all for everything. The genuine love and support you have shown over the years has been invaluable. I know I have not always made the best decisions but you never stop speaking life into me. To my Auntie Tanya, who is in heaven; thank for always taking the time to do my hair.

It didn't matter if I had braids or dreads, you never said no. To my Uncle Yane, who is in heaven; thank you for teaching me to always stick with family no matter what and for introducing me to 2Pac music. Every time I listen to his music I think about you. To my Uncle Charles; thanks for teaching me how to tint windows. Every summer I knew I had a way to make some money because of you.

To my sisters and my brothers: thank you all for always believing in me and staying solid. You always supported me in whatever I would do. When I used to rap, you knew all of my songs. Cuss words and all. Now that we all are grown, I'm thankful our relationships are still strong. To my nieces and nephews: I'm thankful to be here to see you all grow up and become our future leaders. I want you to know that greatness is inside of you so embrace it and walk in confidence. I believe in you all.

To my male cousins, you know who you are: thank you for always riding. Every-time things got real in the streets you were all on the front line with me. I thank God for seeing us through those times.

I would like to pay tribute to Havana, FL (the home-team), my other family members, friends, teachers, coaches, and the Havana Police Department (HPD). Thank you for the many lessons you taught me. I also appreciate the streets, the struggle, the hard times, the good, the bad, and the ugly because all of it helped make me a better man.

To my classmates: East Gadsden class of 2005: thank you for the love. Thank you for acknowledging the change and growth I have made over the years. You all know first hand how I used to be.

To my church family, colleagues, fraternity brothers, and supporters: thank you for believing in my vision. I appreciate the encouraging messages on social media, the shares, the likes, the calls, and text messages. Thank you for being full of cheer and always in good spirits. Your positive energy gave me the extra strength I needed to get this book finished.

My prayers are with you all. May God continue to bless every one of you. I pray you will be blessed with good health, prosperity, wealth, knowledge, self-discipline, love, peace, joy, and happiness. Most importantly, I pray God uses each of you to show others how good He is and that He's still in the life saving and blessing business.

> *"Nobody can go back and start a new beginning, but anyone can start today and make a new ending".*
>
> ~ **Maria Robinson**

Introduction

What is Breaking Cycles?

"Maintaining love of thousands, and forgiving wickedness, rebellion, and sin. Yet He does not leave the guilty unpunished; he punishes the children and their children for the sin of the parents to the third and fourth generation."

Exodus 34:7

Breaking cycles can be defined as being committed to not repeating the same hindering generational ways of life, habits, behaviors, or routines that have affected many of our family members. Breaking cycles involves sacrifice, dedication, discipline, determination, consistency, courage, and a lot of faith, to name a few. Just like so many others, I too am from a dysfunctional family. I have experienced or witnessed so many bad decisions, mistakes, fear mindsets, and wasted opportunities. The choice not to participate in unhealthy behaviors that you see and are surrounded by daily is a constant battle. Studies have shown that human behavior is largely determined by two things: our parents and our environment. Therefore, it is extremely easy and common for people to inherit traits, characteristics, and self-limiting beliefs that steal their hopes, dreams, goals, and eventually their lives while allowing generational cycles or curses to continue. After reading this book you will understand that you are the cycle breaker in your family. You will identify and defeat those generational cycles to keep them from continuing through future generations, especially your children and grandchildren. You already have all the tools needed to break the cycles in your family. Everything you need is already inside of you. It is already in your heart and your DNA. However, you are responsible for developing and using your skills, your talents, as well as your God-given gifts. The truth is, only you can do it. No one can do it for you. You have to want it. That's a decision that you will have to make and be willing to put in the work it takes to achieve it. This book will help you recognize that everything in life happens for a reason. We just have to embrace it, learn from it and never give up. I'm here to tell you, giving up is not an option and it is not a part of my heritage or yours. If you don't break the cycle it will only continue to affect more generations. It is your choice!

There are so many things that can negatively impact us. Pick one: lack of education, lack of financial literacy, lack of financial independence, single-parent household, mass incarceration, and other legal issues, negative influences, being in debt, poverty, on welfare, drugs and alcohol addictions, drug dealing, health-related issues, family holding grudges against family, poor communication skills, domestic violence, having kids early, verbal and sexual abuse, homosexuality, divorce, adultery, depression, lying, laziness, gambling, anger, behavioral issues, mental and physical sicknesses, lack of life insurance, and the list goes on and on. Once you recognize what the generational cycles are in your family that need to be broken, start praying for the self-discipline, strength, and the courage you need to break them. The change you want to see in your family and your life starts with you! I never said it would be easy but I can tell you this, with God on your team you are off to a great start and the odds are in your favor. He has the power to change things, circumstances, and lives.

"If you change the way you look at things, the things you look at change.

~ Wayne Dyer

CHAPTER **ONE**

"Know Yourself"

"For every choice you make, there is a consequence to face. Choose Wisely!"

~ *Kemi Sogunle*

Havana, Florida (Gadsden County) is where my story begins. Small little town with only two traffic lights, and only one grocery store. Growing up in Havana, my family lived below the poverty line. My neighborhood was impoverished; we did not have a lot to do but that was all I knew for a very long time. I love my home-town because it taught me to work hard. It taught me that nobody was going to give me anything. It also taught me that there are no handouts, and life is not fair. It taught me that I had to go and get for myself the life I wanted to live. Most importantly, it taught me how to survive. I'm my mama's first child and only son. I'm named after my daddy because at the time my parents thought I was his first child and first son. We later found out that I had an older brother when I was in the sixth grade. I may not be my dad's first son but I got most of his characteristics. I look like my daddy, I act like my daddy, and I talk like my daddy. Growing up I wanted to be a hustler, a "dope boy" just like my daddy and I almost went down the same prison path just like my daddy. Together my parents had four children including me. My dad also gave me two brothers and a sister not from my mom. What can I say; daddy was a rolling stone!

Growing up my family bounced around from this house to that house throughout the town of Havana. Nonetheless, I spent the first several years of my childhood in Havana Height Apartments, apt. H-1. "The PJ's", Project babies' is how society refers to us. Underprivileged is how we were classified. The ghetto or section 8 is what some call it. But, that's not who I am just because some people may call or try to categorize me as that. I'm much more than what some may think of me and you are too. One of the most important things in life is what you think about yourself. Do you believe in yourself? Self-confidence and self-belief were imperative for me trying to survive in the streets and make it out of the struggle. It wasn't important what others believed or thought about me. I was too focused on what I had to do for myself. I had no time to worry about other people's opinions. My dad always told me "son people are going to talk about you whether you are doing good or bad, so do good and give them something to talk about".

So, who am I? Without my first and last name to identify me, without my titles, without having self-awareness and self-knowledge of who I am, without knowing how precious and how loved I am, all I am and all I will become is a product of my environment and a reflection of the individuals I affiliate with. However, in reality, most of the world will see me as just another black man. Honestly, not much would separate me from being just another typical black man or from having a felony on my record or being in prison, or 6 feet in the ground like so many others. So, what is it that distinguishes me from being just another black man or just another statistic? I was also raised in low-income housing "The Projects", my father spent about 14 years of my childhood in and out of Federal or State prison forcing my mama to occupy the role of a single parent. I was only a baby,10 months when my pop was sentenced to 7 years in federal prison and 2 years on probation. My mama did what she had to do to provide. My family sometimes struggled to make ends meet in my household. We had to get government assistance and go without most of our wants. But, my mama made sure we had what we needed. Therefore, who am I?

What I just described could be most of the males I know, most of all my cousins, and maybe some of yours too. Over time I learned it was what was inside of me that made me different. I did not have the spirit of fear in me. This helped me to rise above my circumstances. Despite what my situation looked like growing up, I chose to better my life by working hard and getting a quality education. I was willing to sacrifice. However, I had to learn self-discipline. I was strong-minded, resilient, and courageous.

I made many mistakes but I learned from them and attempted not to repeat the same ones. I made it out of the streets. I came from the bottom and I beat the odds! I am the first male in my family to graduate from college. Growing up I didn't know what an HBCU (Historically Black College or University) was. Now I am a proud FAMU alum. So, who am I? I am just a living testimony of how good God is. I am a generational cycle breaker and you are too.

How well do you know yourself? Are you self-confident, do you make good decisions, are you disciplined, are you a hard worker? On the other hand, are you unsure of who you are, have you already stopped believing in yourself, have some of your bad choices caused you to lose hope and give up on yourself? I'm asking you these questions because success or failure starts with you. The better you know yourself, the better understanding you will have of what you are capable of doing. One day you will find yourself face to face with a particular situation and you will know for a fact there is no way you are going to make it through it. I'm here to tell you until you know and trust God, you will never fully know yourself or unlock all the greatness that is already inside of you. Life is unpredictable but God's promise is forever and unchanging. I'm certain in who I am because I am sure of who God is. The kind of faith and dependence I have in God comes from trials and tribulations. It comes from many years of wrongdoing, many months of not knowing how I would make it and many days of fearing failure. My life struggles didn't force me to quit on myself but it pushed me closer to God. My adversities helped shape me into the man I am today. They have motivated me to break the generational cycles in my family. Your hard times, your struggles, and disappointments are doing the same for you. So, trust God and trust the process. You are chosen to do an assignment that only you can do. So, how bad do you want it? How well do you know yourself? How much do you love yourself? Success or failure - it's a choice, it's your choice.

How strong is your belief in yourself? What's your personality? Are you a pleasant person to be around? Do you get angry or cop an attitude easily? Do you treat others the way you want to be treated? These are simple questions about you. Sometimes you have to look at yourself in the mirror and ask yourself, am I getting in my way, am I truly applying myself to my full potential, am I living out my purpose in life? For me, those were some tough questions, but I had to look myself in the eyes and be real and honest with myself. For me to learn myself, to learn self-discipline, and to learn how to truly believe in myself. I had to go through a lot. But I had to learn how to trust God. I trusted me and I did what I wanted to do. I had to learn that God is in me and I had to believe that He has a greater purpose for my life. For many years I was blind, and I had two functioning eyes. But I was living with no purpose because I was walking by sight only. I had very little faith. I did not know myself. I was becoming the person I wanted to be and not who God intended me to be. Once I placed God as the head of my life, that's when I was ultimately able to start learning my true identity. So, I'll ask you again. How well do you know yourself? In other words, how well do you know the God in you? God is real! Get to know Him and He will reveal to you who you are. You are a child of God.

We have different gifts, according to the grace given to each of us. If your gift is prophesying, then prophesy in accordance with your faith; if it is serving, then serve; if it is teaching, then teach; if it is to encourage, then give encouragement; if it is giving, then give generously; if it is to lead, do it diligently; if it is to show mercy, do it cheerfully.
Romans 12:6-8

CHAPTER **TWO**

"Educate Yourself"

"Without education, you are not going anywhere in this world."

~ Malcolm X

Without my education, where would I be? Some people can only imagine how different my life would be. However, I can visualize how different my life would have been. All I have to do is recall my life experiences. *"Experience: the most brutal of teachers. But you learn, my God do you learn"* (C.S. Lewis). Growing up in poverty, my mindset was survival by any means necessary. My hood and my cousins taught me to be tough. Watching my mama struggle taught me to work hard. One of the characteristics that were natural for me was paying attention. I was very observant and I saw how the lack of education affected so many of my family members.

The biggest factor was the lack of jobs or the inability to get quality employment. Most of my family members are very hard workers. They are survivors. They do what they have to do to make it through. But because they lacked a solid education or only had a high school diploma, general education diploma (GED), or no college education, the types of employers that would hire them were very limited. I recognized this at an early age and noticed the difference between my family and some of my friends' families. They appeared to be living better from the outside looking in. As I got older I found that one major difference was the level of education. My mama did not finish high school because she gave birth to me at the beginning of her senior year. She stopped attending school because she had to be a mother. I wondered why my mama would always say to me "you will graduate high school" all the time. It was because she never did. She was planting the seed in me then to break that cycle. But, she never mentioned anything about going to college. I also wondered about that. My mama did the best she could with what she had and what she knew. How could she talk about or expose me to college when she never went or had any college exposure? It is a generational cycle. I feel that if most people could have their way, all parents would want their children to have more and live a better life than they were able to live. However, that's not reality. In my reality, there are two or three generations of immediate families and family members that are living in the same public housing apartments today. "Stay Woke"! I am breaking this cycle in my family. I am a college-educated man and I am sure that is one reason why I am living the life I am. It is not because I did anything special. I only took my education a little more seriously than a few of my relatives and peers. School was easy for me and as a plus, all the girls were in school so I did not mind going at all! I also give my mama credit for that because she made sure I was in school every day. She knew I had to get an education to even stand a chance of making it in this world. I will never forget when I went back to my hometown (Havana, FL) for a Northside High School mega reunion a few years ago. While there I ran into my childhood friend, who is more like family now. As we were talking and telling old stories going down memory lane, he said something so profound to me. He said, "my guy you made it out, you did it". He went on to say, "you and I did most of the same things growing up in these streets but, I am a convicted felon and you are a teacher." His last words were "out of all the stuff we done out here in these streets, you never stop going to school". That conversation looped through my mind the entire 2-hour drive back home to Jacksonville, FL. I realized he was correct. Because I did not give up on my education, it paid off for me. So, I want to encourage you to not give up on your education. Whether it's high school, college, graduate school, trade school, truck school, culinary school, or cosmetology school, please do not give up on your dreams. When you give up on your dreams you give up on the opportunities to break cycles in your family. Neither you nor I can see the future but I am one of the thousands of cycle breakers that will tell you that in most cases your level of education is tied to your level of success.

Let me be clear when I say educate yourself. It is not always going to come from school or a teacher. Educating yourself will come from different places, people and different times of our lives. For example, when growing up I was more concerned with making money than making a high-Grade Point Average (GPA). I was more focused on having street credit than establishing a line of credit. I learned how to survive on the streets. Street knowledge can-not be obtained from a college. God knew what I needed to go through to be better prepared for Him to use me. The good news is He knows exactly what you need too.

We all will have different journeys in life, different knowledge, different teachers, different struggles, but the same Father. God will direct our paths to help educate us. Some lessons may be more difficult than others but, that's life. For example, when I was sixteen I was arrested and I knew it was not a joke and that was not the life I wanted for myself. I knew I had to make better choices so I would not find myself back in that situation. For my father, brother, cousins and a lot of my friends, it took a few more times for them to learn the lesson God was trying to teach them. Sometimes God will place you in a situation where you can not call on anybody for help but Him. He has a way of educating you so that lesson will never be forgotten. Although God gives every one of us a brain, we are all different. Therefore, we all learn differently. It takes some people longer to learn than others. I remember being in high school and I had a few honors classes with the smart kids. Even though I was in this prestigious class with all the high performing students, we all learned differently. For example, after most new lessons the teacher would ask the class, "does anyone have any questions about the new material we just went over before we move on". If a student or students needed more help the teacher would allow the rest of the class who understood the lesson to move on and work independently on something else while he went back and retaught that same lesson again but in a slightly different way for the other students. That is the same thing God is doing in our lives. He knows how long it will take you to get it, how many times it will take you to get it, and the situations He has to place you in to allow the knowledge to stick. When you educate yourself, you have knowledge that can never be taken away from you. Some of the knowledge we need to break cycles will not come from a book or a university but life experiences. Some lessons are not taught, but simply must be lived. The lesson of seeing your mama work hard day in and day out just to provide for you and your sisters can-not be taught. The lesson of hearing a policeman, tell you to your face as a teenager that you will be just like your daddy, sell drugs and end up in prison can not be taught. The lesson of having to bury your cousins and friends at young ages can not be taught. The lesson and the anxiety of being robbed with two loaded guns pointed in your face can not be taught. The lesson and the emotions you feel when your house has just been shot up and one of the bullets just barely missed your sister sitting in the kitchen can not be taught. I had to experience all of these lessons. If I hadn't, I would not understand the generational cycles that God intended for me to break. We all have heard the phrase, "everything happens for a reason". That is so true, so do not feel like you are unqualified because you may be going through a tough lesson right now. God is allowing you to become educated in that area because He knows how that knowledge will assist you later in your life. Just because you did not learn your last lesson the teacher is still willing to take you through a remedial course. So, you can not give up. It is your choice but it is a choice you must make every day. Stay focused on God the teacher and He will make sure the lesson is eventually learned.

"Education is the passport to the future, for tomorrow belongs to those who prepare for it today".
~ *Malcolm X*

CHAPTER **THREE**

"Be Patient"

"We don't receive wisdom; we must discover it for ourselves after a journey that no one can take for us or spare us".

~ *Marcel Proust*

have done many things that I am not proud of. But what do you tell a 14-year-old boy who is hustling in the streets to help his mother because he is too young to get a legitimate job? What do you say to a boy when his father is in prison and the only male role models he has are his older cousins and homeboys up the road, and most of them had a black or blue flag hanging out their pocket, selling drugs, smoking weed, and drinking MD 20/20? What do you say to a teenage boy who has adult responsibilities at home? There is not a lot you can say, especially if you can not relate to what that young man is going through. But, my experiences help me to relate to the young people who find themselves in these exact types of situations. I can say to them, you got this! Just keep moving your feet, just keep going. *"Trust in the Lord with all your heart; and do not depend on your own understanding. Seek his will in all you do, and he will show you which path to take"* (Proverbs 3:5-6). To change your life, you first must change your mindset. Stop looking at your life through a straw and start looking at your life through a magnifying glass. Get focused and zoom in on your life. In other words, look at your life with a bigger vision. Understand that life has its seasons just like the weather. For instance, at different times throughout the year, we experience different seasons. The wet autumn (fall), the dry spring, the summer heat, and even the winter cold. Each season brings different types of conditions. We have to apply that same perspective to our lives. At different times throughout our lives, we will have different seasons. For example, sometimes we hit hard patches and we struggle, sometimes we are blessed with a little extra and we splurge, sometimes we are happy and vibrant, and other times we may be sad and grieving. Whatever season you are in right now, I want you to look at the bigger picture and appreciate the process. Find the positive in that season because it could have been worse. By going through these different seasons we are better equipped and prepared for our journeys in life. Everything in life happens for a purpose. However, it does not happen according to my timetable or yours. We the people must learn to be patient in all things. Growing up I wanted money and I wanted it fast. I wanted to end my family struggles because I saw the stress, depression, and frustration it caused. What I did not see at the time was how I would benefit from the struggle. The smell of kerosene heaters during the winter, using the oven to heat the house, having to boil water to take a bath, killing roaches every day, and the arguments and fist-fights I witnessed between my parents seemed unfair. However, those experiences became the fuel that pushed me to break those cycles so my kids would not have to experience the same things. What I am telling you is try to find the good even in a negative situation. Almost every successful individual I have been blessed to meet, have all had different but very similar stories. They had to sacrifice for many years before they were able to live the life they had always wanted. Be patient and wait on your turn! Sometimes you have to be happy for somebody else before your blessing shows up. Sometimes it takes being connected to the right person. Sometimes you just have to wait on God. To become a cycle breaker, you must understand that patience is essential. You cannot change your family overnight. But, by making the daily decision to work toward your goals and never give up, eventually, you will see all your hard work begin to pay off. This will help you to take your life to higher destinations while breaking cycles at the same time.

Nowadays we live in a microwave society. Nobody wants to wait for anything. We want what we want and we want it right now. Social media is a huge reason for this because we see our friends and other individuals we follow posting their best moments and we want that for ourselves and our families. Believe me, I get it. Everybody wants money in the bank, a retirement account, a nice big house, car, clothes, shoes, and jewelry. We want to travel the world but we do not want to be patient enough to wait on God for it. While growing up, my dad would tell me stories and show me pictures about what he used to do and used to have. It was not until I was older when I realized that my pops did not wait on God either. Because what God has for you no man can take it away. My pops lost it all because he wanted to do it his way on his own time. However, like so many, my pops who also grew up without his father. My grandfather was shot and killed when my dad was just a child. My dad did what he did to try to provide a better life for himself. My dad was trying to break cycles and he may have. But what he did not see was by doing it his way, he was also starting new cycles. He was trying to break cycles his way and not God's way. God gives us all free will, the freedom to make our own choices. That's a big responsibility and it is not as simple as it sounds. Making good choices comes with time. Do you ever wonder why as a kid our parents made most of our major decisions for us? Yep, you got it. Because our parents or guardians knew we were not mentally prepared to make certain decisions on our own because our brains were not fully developed. However, over time, day by day, year after year, we begin to grow up. As we grow older we should gain wisdom. This process also happens over time. We have to be patient. Even when we are adults God knows that we are still not ready to make all of our decisions because we are not spiritually mature enough. As our heavenly Father, He is always there to help us. The problem is we think we can do it all on our own and on our timeline. My daddy did it, I did it and you may have done it or are doing it too. For any cycle to be broken in our families, we have to trust God's timing. Grant it, it is not always easy to trust and wait on God. That is why *we walk by faith, not by sight* (2 Corinthians 5:7). Do not let the things of this world rush you because they are not going to rush God. Your blessing may not show up when you want it, but it will always be right on time. Be patient and trust God!

CHAPTER **FOUR**

"Your Decisions"

"Your joy comes from how you think, the choices that we make in life".

~ *Joyce Meyer*

Every day we are tasked with a very difficult job. That job is being a good decision-maker. Growing up I made some bad decisions. I kept trying to go left, even when I knew I should be going right. See it's different when you do not know better, but I knew better. My dad would tell me over and over again, "son slipping doesn't count". It took me years to realize all my dad was saying in his way was son make good decisions. My daddy knew what happened to his life when he got caught making a bad decision and he wanted to protect me. Sometimes the Lord will allow us to get caught in the middle of a bad decision so we can learn from that decision. When we are blessed to make it through our bad decisions, we sometimes think we did something special to get ourselves out of that situation and we go back and try it again. That is exactly what I did. When God was working miracles in my life, I thought it was me working magic. I thought I was better, smarter, or slicker than the police when the officer did not find the drugs I had on me during a traffic stop. I thought it was my good driving skills that kept me from getting seriously hurt in my first serious car accident at the age of 15 when I didn't even have learners permit. I thought a defected bullet was the reason why I didn't accidentally shoot my homeboy Kevin in the stomach while showing him my new .22 rifle when we were teenagers.

At age 19, I was life-flighted by the paramedics to Tallahassee Memorial Hospital unconscious because of a bad ATV 4-wheeler accident I was involved in. The Doctor thought I had severe head trauma and internal bleeding because I was not wearing a helmet and I went through an all brick mailbox. But, once I regained consciousness, displayed that I was competent by answering a few questions, and all my tests cleared, I was able to go home the same night. I had a lot of scrapes and bruises but only a few lacerations to my head and hands. The doctor said I was extremely lucky. Ironically, I thought the same. At the time I did not see it but God was trying to slow me down. He wanted to get my full attention before my bad decisions caused me my freedom or even worse, my life. This accident caused me to withdraw from all my classes I was enrolled in at Tallahassee Community College, at the time. What should have been only one semester off turned into an entire year off? I almost gave up on school. During that time off, my life got harder. I had to work all types of day labor jobs just to make it through the week. I had to take risks in the streets. I had to hustle harder. I had to survive. The student loan financial lenders started to harass me about repaying my loans because I was no longer enrolled in school. See the Lord needed me to be at a very low point for a while in my life. He needed to make it very plain and clear to me that if I did not decide to take control of my life I was going to fall into the same generational cycles that trapped so many of my relatives. He needed me to get focused. The Lord needed me to grow up. I had to make some serious decisions about my life, by myself, and on my own. I decided I wanted more out of life. I decided to try something different. If I would have kept doing the same thing, the same way, I would have kept getting the same results. I couldn't keep waiting around for someone else to push me to my goals. I couldn't expect someone else to believe in my visions when they did not know my story. I made the decision not to stay down, but to get back up, to keep trying, and this time I would try things God's way, not mine.

Let me ask you this. What type of person are you? Are you a leader, or are you a follower? Do you make your decisions based on what gives you a better opportunity to be successful, happy or free? Do you base your decisions on getting love, respect, or validation from the streets, your peers, or your followers? I have been both a follower and a leader. *"He who cannot be a good follower cannot be a good leader"* (Aristotle). I quickly realized that it was not a bad thing that I was being a follower. It was more the people, the habits, the spirits that I decided to follow. For example, I associated myself with gangsters and hustlers; so it was only a matter of time before I was hustling. However, if I would have associated myself with young achievers who had success plans and goals for their lives; soon I would have started making success plans and goals for my own life. I wasted several years of my life living without a purpose. I had no plans or goals so my life was stuck in neutral day after day. Nevertheless, because of all the different seasons and experiences I have had, I developed a good work ethic. I learned that everybody that smiled in my face and every hand I shook did not genuinely want me to be great. The most important aspect I learned from the different seasons in my life was through it all the Lord never left my side. So many times I had to face difficult circumstances but because of all of the prior difficult seasons in my life, I was more equipped to deal with the new ones. This gave me the hope and confidence to keep striving to become a better man and to break the cycles in my family. I decided to believe in myself knowing that no one else could do it for me. I had to trust God, be confident in myself, in my visions, and all my endeavors. I had no one else to depend on but me. I also had no one else to blame but me for my decisions and I was up for the challenge. *"If you have no confidence in self, you are twice defeated in the race of life"* (Marcus Garvey).

Growing up I had no clue how my life would turn out as many of us do not. I did not fully understand how powerful and strong the human mind is. We all can remember at least one teacher or one person telling us "you can do anything you set your mind too". In other words, you can do anything you decide to do with your life but you are the one that must do it. Honestly, I did not believe that growing up. It did sound like a good phrase for my teachers, coaches, and the preachers to use. Today, I am living what I once called the dream life. The wife, kids, and house with the white fence. More importantly, I am spiritually, mentally, and physically healthy. Even though I am not where I need to be, I am still very grateful I am not where I used to be. My life changed because I decided to follow God. I stopped doing what I wanted to do and started letting God guide my steps. In this present day, I can say with conviction that you truly can do and become anything you set your mind too. You can be the first in your family to learn how to save and invest your money and you can break the cycle of lacking financial literacy. You can be the first business owner in your family breaking the cycle of always working for someone else. You can be the first health enthusiast in your family and break the cycle of being overweight or obese which leads to other health issues. It starts in your mind and you must believe it in your heart. You have to make the decision that you can do it and you are going to do it. Only you can make the decision that you will be successful. Your mama, your daddy not even your teacher, or your preacher can make that decision for you. They can pray for you, encourage, and support you along the way, but you are the one who has to put in the work.

I asked myself the same question; who am I? Because of some fairly good decision making, today I am someone who chose not to give up on my goals. As a result, I did not forfeit my future. Despite all of the injustice I witnessed in my community, I refused to allow my surroundings to dictate the outcome of my life. The police misconduct, the black on black crimes, the hate amongst family members, and so much more was disheartening. I realized the kind of life I wanted to live was in my hands and I did not want to fumble it. I saw what happened to my friends, cousins, uncles, brother, and my father when they fumbled their lives for just a moment. The judicial system picked it up, and now in some form or fashion still has some control over their lives. *"If you are born poor its not your mistake, but if you die poor its your mistake"* (Bill Gates Sr.).

I have lived most of my life in poverty. I was born into it. I had no say so in that matter. So, I lived the life I was given. In spite of that, I never stop trying to better myself, never stop trying to improve my living conditions. I never stop trying to make my mama proud of me. *"If at first you don't succeed, try, try, try, try, try again"* (Michael Chang). Nothing in life worth having comes easy, so I would imagine everyone would be successful, thriving, and living their best life. Since we all know that is not the case, what decisions are you making today to ensure that you do not waste your life and allow the generational cycles to be sustained? It is your life, and it is your decision!

> *"If you're walking down the right path and you're willing to keep walking, eventually you'll make progress."*
>
> *~ Barack Obama*

CHAPTER **FIVE**

"Be Strong Minded"

"Be strong minded, and always believe that the impossible is possible".

~ *Selena*

L ike myself, a lot of men and women work out, jog, or partake in some type of exercise activity. The reason why we do this is to keep ourselves fit and in shape so our hearts and bodies can operate at the most effective levels. Therefore, we watch the types and amounts of food we intake. We even are aware of the liquids we consume. This takes a lot of discipline. Many successful people have this trait. They are also usually strong-minded individuals. Being strong-minded is another way to describe being mentally tough. Being disciplined and resilient enough to rebound from childhood hardships, the disappointment of an absent parent, or even just the traumas of life are examples of a strong-minded person. In life, there will come a time when each person will face something that will shake them up or turn their lives upside down. I have been experiencing adversity all my life, and even as an adult it still shows up. Mishaps and hard times are things we can not avoid. However, you can prepare for adversity. Preparation is quite simple and no it is not just saving money, because believe it or not, there are something's even money can't fix. Let's not get it confused; having money saved up is a great thing and it definitely will benefit you on your road to breaking generational cycles. However, money can-not save our loved ones from death.

My wife and I lost our six-month-old baby girl Malia Dionne Bunion to the worst disease you never heard of called Epidermolysis Bullosa, also known as EB. Going through that not only tested how strong my mind was but more importantly how strong my faith was. For a moment I questioned God, I even questioned my faith. How and why is this happening to my daughter, to me and my family? I did not understand it. However, because I had a relationship with God I was able to see how He was still in control even in my darkest moment. I was able to hear Him when He answered my questions. I prayed every day "God please don't let my baby suffer!" "God take the pain away from her and give it to me!" He answered my prayers. If she had lived, she would have been in constant pain. My sweet baby is no longer in pain. God heard little ole me. Many people were quick to say "I do not know how you are being so strong because I would lose my mind". Believe me, losing a child is by far the most difficult pain I have ever had to endure and many may not understand it unless you have walked in those shoes. When we know God for real, then you know that when we are at our weakest point that's when He's at His strongest. Through all my trials and tribulations, I can say that being strong-minded is based on having a strong faith. Having a strong faith, you will discover strength inside of you that you didn't know existed. Just like we spend time in the gym training our bodies we have to spend time praying and meditating with God to train our mind. Living in this world, there are many distractions and they can easily devour our attention from what we need to be doing. Stay focused on your goals and what is important before you find yourself in a state of captivity. Do not allow society, social media, your cellular phone, reality television, your past, or what you may be dealing with right now keep your mind caged. The frame of mind of your family can be renovated by you. When Malia died, my wife and our two other kids were watching me and feeding off of my energy. I had to be strong. Just like you have to be strong. You have to train your mind to focus on the positives and do not dwell on the negatives. The stronger your faith is in God, the stronger your mind will be. In my opinion, they go hand and hand. I have dealt with tons of heartaches in my life and the only reason why I did not lose myself is because of my faith in the Lord. Being a cycle breaker comes with some disappointments, failures, disapprovals, frustrations, even moments where you feel you are alone and it's you against the world. All of these are normal emotions and feelings. Going through these difficult stages in life is going to push you. You can allow them to push you to drugs, push you to stress, push you to depression, push you to the streets, push you to illegal activities, or you can allow them to push you closer to God. Spending more time getting to know God will strengthen your faith. It will also strengthen your mind to be able to continue the marathon of life and to remain on the mission of breaking the generational cycles in your family. God is the source of love, peace, and happiness. When He gives us strength we will be able to live victoriously in any situation and make it through any problem.

> "You never know how strong you are until being strong is your only choice".
>
> ~ *Bob Marley*

CHAPTER **SIX**

"Stay Hungry for More"

"The tragedy of life is often not in our failure, but rather in our complacency; not in our doing too much, but rather in our doing too little; not in our living above our ability, but rather in our living below our capacities."

~ Benjamin E. Mays

To be honest, coming from Havana, FL, being in these streets, doing the things I have done, and seeing the things I have seen, I could easily settle and be satisfied right where I am in life. I could get a big head. I could have that "I made it out so I'm not worried about nobody else" attitude. But, that is not who I am. See, I am very proud of myself considering where I started and how far I have made it despite all the obstacles. I am only doing what a man is supposed to be doing. That's trying to be the best example of what a man is and taking care of my family. It's still so much work to be done and so many cycles to be broken. Therefore, I stay humble but stay hungry. This is what I often tell myself as a reminder because I can not afford to get too comfortable where I am in life and neither can you.

When you are on an assignment to break generational cycles and to show your family, friends, and community that change is possible and there's a better way, you have to expect prosperity. Do not be stunned when the blessing is greater than what you prayed for. When you are a cycle breaker you are going to reach higher levels and do things that many others in your family may not have. This does not mean you should get comfortable. God has to bless some of us in small doses because He knows if we get too much money too fast, some of us won't know how to act. He sees how some of us act right now with the little blessings. When we work hard and sacrifice for years, it will not be in vain. You have to know that so, you do not lose your passion for life. Just embrace that you are right where God intends for you to be and keep pressing forward. The word of God tells us to trust Him. When you trust Him, then you will believe in what He said; *"I have come that they may have life, and that they may have it more abundantly"* (John 10:10). I am a living testament that when God is involved things change. My life has changed for the better. I have new opportunities, new favor, new neighbors, new hope, and most importantly a new mindset. What has not changed is my appetite for more. I give all praise to God for what I have and I am grateful for it. On the other hand, God does not intend for us to forget about the things He has brought us through. I still remember precisely the times when I had nothing; nothing but uncertainty. I was uncertain of how I would be able to provide for myself. I now understand how easily and expeditiously my life could be different. We all are one bad decision, one mistake, or one slip up away from being back at square one. It's a scary reality. For this reason, I stay hungry for more. *"Your previous accomplishments should be your stepping stones; you need them to jump up. They should not become beds that should keep you comfortably sleeping"* (Israelmore Ayivor).

Nowadays we have so many distractions. For example, social media is distracting so many people from reality. Some people are so concerned with what's going on in someone else's life, that they can not get their own lives in order. Social media has a lot of people hungry for attention instead of being hungry for a better life, a better way. Stay focused on your life goals. Stay hungry for more even if you feel like you are already doing pretty good. It does not matter where you currently are in life, you can be better. You have to understand that people do not know your struggles and how hard you had to work to have what you have. So do not be distracted and get comfortable, stay hungry!

Growing up I figured out as a teenager that nobody was going to take care of me the way I was going to take care of myself. I knew if I did not work, I did not eat. If I got in a jam, who could I call? This was my life. That's a lot of pressure on a young man but, diamonds are made from high heat and intense pressure. Nothing worth having comes easy, it comes with a price. We live in a "more and more" society. Everybody wants more money, cars, popularity, followers, and more likes. In other words, people are hungry for more but they are hungry for more of the wrong things. They are searching for more in all of the wrong places. When our bodies are hungry we eat. Food provides us with essential nutrients, which is our main source of energy. So, when our life is hungry for more we have to do the same thing and go to the main source of energy. What I am saying is we have to have a desire and a hunger to know God. *"I can do all things through Christ who strengthens me"* (Philippians 4:13).

When you connect with God, some of the things you are craving, for now, will stop and He will give you a craving for something new.

Since I was a teenager I've been chasing paper. I was so hungry for more money because I saw how important it was. Growing up in the streets of Havana, I noticed some very distinct differences between the haves and the have not's. When you had money you had respect and a voice in the streets and the communities. Without money, you were a bum. The streets would treat you like an outcast if you had nothing. It was not about how old you were; it was about that dollar bill. At age 16, I was a man. I hung with people that were grown so I was involved in grown people activities. I was smoking, drinking, and partying in my hometown club L&J's on Sunday nights and I had school the next day. This was the norm in my hood. We grew up fast and it felt like we did not have any choice but to. It was a cycle. I was only doing what I thought I had to do to make it out of the hood. But what I was doing was going to keep me in the hood. I put my trust in the streets and not in the Savior. I leaned on my cousins for help, not Christ. I was going to clubs but not church. I was looking up to gangsters but not God. Despite all the wrong I was doing, the Lord still had mercy on me.

In 2004, I was handcuffed and locked up for the first time as a teenager. I had a warrant for my arrest for a fight I was involved in. My first night in that cell alone I stayed up thinking and praying. Once the door shut I had to face reality. I thought about my dad who was already in prison at the time. I knew he would be mad and disappointed in me because my dad would always tell me, "son slipping out here in these streets does not count". In other words, one mess up and your entire life can be changed. And at that moment I felt like I had slipped. My dad would write me letters all the time telling me to slow down, I was moving too fast. He would tell me "I'm doing prison time so my son wouldn't have to". I did not listen to my dad because he would tell me all these things but he was not there to show me what I should be doing and how I should be doing it. Yet, my dad was right. While I was trying to be just like my daddy, my dad wanted me to be hungry for more and to learn from his mistakes.

I felt alone, low, embarrassed, and the only thing I could do was pray. It was funny because when I was free I wouldn't call on God for anything. I thought it was all me. However, it was my first night locked up and I was praying asking Him for help. I thought all I needed was money. But God knew exactly what I had to go through for Him to reach me. The whole time I was running the streets hungry for more money, I should have been running to the sanctuary hungry for more of the Master. He is the One who provides all of our needs. I was mentally lost and was drifting through life without a plan. After a day or two I was released, free to go home with a pending court date. What was even more mind-blowing to me was it seemed like the streets respected me more because I had been locked up. My older homeboys and cousins looked at me differently now because I had experienced something that most of them had already been through. I was booked and had an official arrest record. I was in the system. I did not understand my emotions because in my mind I knew I had messed up. But, in the streets, it felt like I was celebrated as if going to jail was cool or normal. It was a cycle. My life was headed down the wrong path. I had to become hungry for more than what my environment offered. I knew I wanted more but I had no clue how to attain it because of the lack of exposure. I was not even sure of what more or a better life looked like. I had to feed my mind with positivity, daily self-encouragement, and with a daily bible scripture for my life to grow and change. I had to redirect my life. When I started to cultivate a hunger to know God better, that's when my hunger to be the best version of myself began. It was hunger to help more people, hunger to take my education seriously, hunger to be more active in church, and hunger to break generational cycles. Every day our bodies need food because we all know the impact it has on our health. But, every day we are not seeking more of God when we all know the impact He can have on our lives. Stay hungry for God and He will use your life to show others how powerful He is. Let that digest!

> *"Every man and woman is born into the world to do something unique and something distinctive and if he or she does not do it, it will never be done".*
>
> ~ *Benjamin E. Mays*

CHAPTER SEVEN

"Embrace your Growth"

"When I was a child, I talked like a child,
I thought like a child, I reasoned like a child.
When I became a man, I put the ways of child-
hood behind me".

1 Corinthians 13:11

The longer we live, the wiser we should become. But that is not always true because I know some old fools and you probably do too. Every birthday we are blessed to see; our age will increase by one. So, physically we are older. In some cases, our body, our appearance, and depending on your age even the color of your hair may change. That's normal, that's life. Nothing is intended to stay the same forever. So, just like our physique grows and changes, what about your mentality? When I say mentality I mean your character, your attitude, your reasoning, your humility, your mental age, your outlook on life. These are attributes that only you will be able to change about yourself. In life, there are some things we have control over and there are some things we simply do not. For example, if you are alive and breathing today, then you must consume the appropriate nutrients to sustain life. We do not have a choice in that matter but we do have a choice in what we eat and what we drink. Once we get a certain age we should understand that our body is going to grow and change regardless. However, it will change based on what we eat and drink. These are choices we have to make. We have no control over what the weather will be daily but we do have the choice over what we will dress ourselves in to be prepared for the day. So my question to you is what kind of choices are you making today to prepare yourself for the growth and changes we all will face in life? Because as you can see your body is going to grow and change whether you want it to or not. However, your mentality will not grow without your diligence. So, do not think just because your birthday is coming up, and your physical body has changed that your mentality has automatically converted or you have automatically matured.

You can go to google and search "how to change or grow my mindset or mentality" and a list of articles and blogs will show up with great suggestions and strategies. But after you try all of those you may still find yourself in the same place where you started. That's exactly what happened to me. I was trying to change my mindset, I was trying to grow as a man, I was trying to get out the streets, I was trying to change my life, but the mistake I was making was "I" was trying to do it on my own. It was not until 2009 when I scheduled a meeting with my Pastor at the time O. Jermaine Simmons of Jacob Chapel Baptist Church in Tallahassee, Florida. During our meeting I explained to him that I was trying to make better decisions, I explained I wanted more for myself, and I knew I needed to grow as a man but I did not know how to do it. In other words, I was trying to break the cycles my life was revolving in. Pastor Simmons allowed me to vent to him and he replied with a typical "pastor" answer. He looked me in my eyes and said, "just keep coming to church, keep trusting God, and everything around you will change." See I missed what Pastor Simmons was saying to me in that meeting. But, I was obedient and kept going to church, kept reading my bible, and kept leaning on and trusting the Lord. What the Pastor was saying to me became clear. I can not change and grow mentally until I grow spiritually. It was not until I was able to embrace and understand the growth I was undergoing spiritually before I was able to embrace and understand the growth I was going through mentally and as a man.

If you want to break generational cycles in your family, you should hope for change and look forward to your personal growth. Because think about it, if you continue to do the same things your parents or relatives did, how can you expect a different outcome for your life? *"The definition of insanity is doing the same thing over and over again, but expecting different results"* (Albert Einstein). If you want to break cycles, you can not be afraid to step out on faith. To have that type of faith, you have to grow spiritually. To grow spiritually, you have to develop a prayer life. Once you grow your prayer life, you will grow your relationship. Once your relationship grows, your faith grows. Once your faith grows, that is when you grow as an individual. Embrace your growth, be patient, and wait on God. I know how bad you want to be successful. I know how bad you want to make your family proud. I know how bad you want to break those generational cycles. But you can not do it alone. Sometimes God will place you around people just to help you grow. Sometimes He intends for us to learn the right way to do certain things, and other times God may need us to learn what not to do. Have you ever asked yourself, why do my friends get in so much trouble? Why are so many of my family members going to jail? Why are so many of my classmates dying so young? Why are so many of these teenage girls getting pregnant? God wants you to pay attention and be observant of what is going on around you because that's His way of showing you what will happen to your life if you do not embrace change and growth in your life.

When I lost my uncle Lamonte (Mont) and my first cousin Montez (Tez) to DOC (the department of corrections), the prison system in the summer of 2007, it impacted me in a major way as a man. My uncle was sentenced to 30 years and my cousin received 25 years. I did not understand it at all. I was puzzled. I was with these guys every day, we did the same things, we broke bread together, we got money together, we were brothers. This situation caused me so much pain, so much frustration, I was broken inside, I was angry, but there was nothing I could do but pray for them and pray for myself. What I did not realize was how this same situation that caused me so much distress would also cause me to grow so much. This situation pushed me closer to God. I know the reason why I was not in the car with them that night was all Him. Second degree attempted murder was the charge. I felt like if only I could have been there that night, things would not have transpired the way they did and my brothers would still be free. Instead, my oldest child is now ten years old and neither one of them has ever met him face to face, never hugged him, and never had the chance to tell him the stories about how we came up. See when things like this happen to other people who you may know but you don't see or talk to every day, you may miss the lesson and the warning God is trying to give to you. Sometimes for some people like myself to truly see the signs and see the forewarning of what path our life is headed, the Lord will allow things to hit close to home. And so, when awful things happen in your life, it is okay to be sad, to be upset, to cry, to grieve, but do not miss the lesson and opportunity for growth that comes from enduring difficult situations. After seeing what happened to my uncle and my cousin I had a serious choice to make. Because I just witnessed where the type of lifestyle we were living leads to 30 years in prison or the cemetery. Therefore, I chose not to quit, not to give up on my life. I used what happened to my brothers to help me embrace the spiritual, mental, and individual growth I had to go through to become a better man. Trying to break generational cycles is not for the weak. You have to be strong. There will be several bumps and detours along the way. But do not give up, you have a lot of generations before you and after you, that's depending on you. So, strengthen your faith and embrace your growth. Do not give up on yourself, do not give up on God, because He won't give up on you!

Change is inevitable, everything changes! The only things that are not growing and changing are things that have died or never had life. Are you only existing or are you living? I'm living and I'm living for God because He died for me and you. I am breaking generational cycles and all the motivation and power I need to keep going is in my testimony. Your testimony is also your strength, so use it. Never let your circumstances define who you are. I believe in you and your ability to change your life. I believe you are the cycle breaker that will change your family forever.

"Change will not come if we wait for some other person or some other time. We are the ones we've been waiting for; we are the change that we seek."
~ Barack Obama

Message to Reader

Dear Reader, I want to thank you for taking the time out of your busy life to read my book. We all have our testimonies and that's your story. I am very humbled you chose to read mine. I am a normal individual just like you. I am just trying to be obedient to our Heavenly Father and do my part while I am on this side of heaven. I believe there are some things in life that we can only accomplish with God's help. One of those things is breaking generational cycles. I encourage you to trust God more but first, you have to get to know God more. I encourage you to pray more and ask Him to guide your life. He will take you to higher levels and open new doors of opportunities. I hope that this book will save lives, change minds, and inspire more people to break those hindering generational cycles in their families. I included some of my favorite bible verses and quotes to help remind you that your sacrifices are all worth it. So, stay on your course and it's okay to slow down, just do not stop. You may not see it now but all of your struggles and hard times are making you a stronger person. Embrace your hardships and know it is only God preparing you for greater. When God is trying to grow you as a person, you will have to let go of some things and some people to grow. In closing, remember change and growth does not come from being comfortable. It comes when you are tired of being uncomfortable in the same cycle. You are a cycle breaker! It's your decision not to repeat the same cycles but there's a calling on your life to break the cycles. Trust the process!

Afterthought

"Making New Cycles"

The title of this book is "Breakin Cycles" because, for so many of us, we have to get rid of bad experiences, bad decisions, and bad cycles. However, as you break bad cycles, it is important to start new cycles. I mentioned that when you have faith in God, and when God sees that you're serious about making a change, He gives you what you need to be successful. One of the things He gives you is new opportunities, new acquaintances, and new exposures.

When I met and eventually married my wife, I had no idea how many doors our marriage would open for me. First, I married into a wonderful, successful family that not only accepted me as I was but also exposed me to life at a different level. Even though my in-laws are successful in their careers and their lives, they carry themselves like regular everyday people. In other words, they have shown me that you can have success, but success does not have to have you. You can have money, but money does not have to own you. I am a better father, husband, and man because of this exposure.

I also became a member of Kappa Alpha Psi Fraternity. I remember a time in my life where I thought being a part of a fraternity was not for me, it was unnecessary, and I was too street for that. However, being a part of this fraternity has exposed me to men who are educated, who are business owners, who are serious about growing both spiritually and economically. It is a new cycle in my life.

As I make new cycles, I've also been to places in the world where I could only imagine I would be just a few years ago. Imagine a kid from a little place like Havana going to places like Montego Bay, Jamaica, or Hawaii. From Havana to Hawaii – two six-letter words that start with "H". But that is where the similarities end.

I am happy that as I break bad cycles in my life, I am starting new and better cycles in the lives of my children. My son has learned how to play the game of golf at an early age. He has been to NFL and NBA games. He has been to Disneyworld multiple times. His first trip to Disneyworld as a child was also my first trip to Disneyworld. But I did not go until I was an adult. I have broken the cycle of not having my father physically present in my life during my early years by making the cycle of being involved in my children's lives. Gymnastics, dance practice, football, basketball, birthday parties, vacations, school events. You name it, and I am there for my children. Making memories and making new cycles.

What I am trying to say is that exposure makes a world of difference. In my early years in Havana, I was not exposed to a whole lot of what the world had to offer. But now, I have seen how big the world is, and how many opportunities there are, even for someone who came from the hood like me. I now know that a whole lot exists for me, my children, and yes even for you. As one bad cycle ends in your life, try to develop a new good cycle. Break bad habits and make good ones. Out with the bad cycles, and in with the new good ones. Giving God all the glory along the way!

Notes

1. See 1 Corinthians 13:7. (NLT)

2. See 1 Corinthians 2:9. (NKJV)

3. Quote by: (Maria Robinson, n.d.)
   Retrieved from http://www.goodreads.com/quotes.

4. See Exodus 34:7.

5. Quote by: (Wayne Dyer, n.d.)
   Retrieved from http://www.brainyquote.com/.

6. Quote by: (Kemi Sogunle, n.d.)
   Retrieved from http://www.goodreads.com/quotes.

7. See Romans 12:6-8. (CEV)

8. Quote by: (Malcolm X, n.d.)
   Retrieved from http:// www.brainyquote.com/.

9. Quote by: (C.S. Lewis, n.d.)
   Retrieved from http://www.goodreads.com/quotes.

10. Quote by: (Malcolm X, n.d.)
    Retrieved from http:// www.brainyquote.com/.

11. Quote by: (Marcel Proust, n.d.)
Retrieved from http:// www.brainyquote.com/.

12. See Proverbs 3:5-6. (NLT)

13. See 2 Corinthians 5:7. (NKJV)

14. Quote by: (Joyce Meyer, n.d.)
Retrieved from http:// www.brainyquote.com/.

15. Quote by: (Aristotle, n.d.)
Retrieved from http://www.goodreads.com/quotes.

16. Quote by: (Marcus Garvey, n.d.)
Retrieved from http:// www.brainyquote.com/.

17. Quote by: (Bill Gates, n.d.)
Retrieved from http://www.goodreads.com/quotes.

18. Quote by: (Michael Chang, n.d.)
Retrieved from http:// www.brainyquote.com/.

19. Quote by: (Barack Obama, n.d.)
Retrieved from http:// www.brainyquote.com/.

20. Quote by: (Selena, n.d.)
Retrieved from http://www.goodreads.com/quotes.

21. Quote by: (Bob Marley, n.d.)
Retrieved from http://www.goodreads.com/quotes.

22. Quote by: (Benjamin E. Mays, n.d.)
Retrieved from http:// www.brainyquote.com/.

23. See John 10:10. (NKJV)

24. Quote by: (Israelmore Ayivor, n.d.)
Retrieved from http://www.goodreads.com/quotes.

25. Quote by: (Benjamin E. Mays, n.d.)
Retrieved from http://www.brainyquote.com/.

26. See 1 Corinthians 13:11. (NIV)

27. Quote by: (Albert Einstein, n.d.)
Retrieved from http://www.quotesyoung.com/.

28. Quote by: (Barack Obama, n.d.)
Retrieved from http://www.brainyquote.com/.

29. http://www.debra.org/

30. See Mark 5:19 (ESV)

Special Tribute

Malia Dionne Bunion

Sunrise
March 30, 2019

Sunset
Sept. 26, 2019

We will never forget the day our baby girl was diagnosed with Junctional Epidermolysis Bullosa (JEB). We had never heard about this condition before her birth.

Epidermolysis Bullosa (EB) is a genetic condition that primarily causes blistering of the skin. The blisters can occur from minor friction or trauma. Patients with EB can suffer from chronic wounds and the disease can be debilitating in some cases. JEB-Herlitz is the most severe type of EB and it affects approximately 1 person per every 3 million people per year in the United States. Currently, there is no cure for EB.

For more information, visit: https://debra.salsalabs.org/inmemoryofmalia/p/inmemoryofmalia/index.html

"Our Sweet Baby"

POEM CREATED BY TONY BUNION, JR.

To Our Sweet Baby Malia,

We are so sorry we couldn't stop your pain,

but our hearts rejoice because we know it wasn't in vain.

We will always call your name

every time we pray and we will always praise God for the time you got to stay.

We will miss staring in your eyes, kissing you on your head, and singing nursery rhymes to you while standing around your bed.

Sleep sweet baby, and don't you worry about a thing all your pain and suffering is over,

Baby Malia, you got your wings...

Love Mom and Dad

A portion of all book sales will be donated to Debra of America, to help find a cure and to help those currently living with EB. *"Because the cost of doing nothing is too great"*.